◢◤ **CORNERSTONES**
◢◤ **OF FREEDOM**™

# Abraham LINCOLN

BY PETER BENOIT

**CHILDREN'S PRESS**®
An Imprint of Scholastic Inc.
New York  Toronto  London  Auckland  Sydney
Mexico City  New Delhi  Hong Kong
Danbury, Connecticut

**BRINGING HISTORY to LIFE**

Content Consultant
James Marten, PhD
Professor and Chair, History Department
Marquette University
Milwaukee, Wisconsin

Library of Congress Cataloging-in-Publication Data

Benoit, Peter, 1955–
    Abraham Lincoln / Peter Benoit.
        p. cm.—(Cornerstones of freedom)
    Includes bibliographical references and index.
    ISBN-13: 978-0-531-25025-9 (lib. bdg.)      ISBN-10: 0-531-25025-3 (lib. bdg.)
    ISBN-13: 978-0-531-26550-5 (pbk.)      ISBN-10: 0-531-26550-1 (pbk.)
    1. Lincoln, Abraham, 1809–1865—Juvenile literature. 2. Presidents—
United States—Biography—Juvenile literature. I. Title.
    E457.905.B4653 2012
    973.7092—dc22 [B]                              2011010823

Photographs © 2012: Alamy Images: 22 (Kim Karpeles), 14, 15, 16, 17, 30
top (North Wind Picture Archives), back cover (Paris Pierce); Clifford
Oliver Photography/www.cliffordoliverphotography.com: 64; Getty
Images/Kean Collection: 20; iStockphoto/DNY59: 6; Jim McMahon: 28;
Library of Congress: 38, 44, 56, 59 top (Mathew Brady), 57 top (Brady-
Handy Collection), 39 (Currier & Ives), 5 left, 32 (Federal Art Project,
WPA), cover, 50 (Alexander Gardner), 24 (L.C. Handy Studios), 57 bottom
(National Photo Company Collection), 26 (Nicholas H. Shepherd), 5 right
(The Thomas Jefferson Papers Series 1), 10, 47, 58 top left; North Wind
Picture Archives: 13 top, 58 top right; ShutterStock, Inc./Ambient Ideas:
2, 3, 54; Superstock, Inc./Currier & Ives: 48; The Art Archive/Picture Desk:
43 (Culver Pictures), 40 (Alexander Gardner/Culver Pictures), 41 (George
Healy/White House, Washington, DC/Superstock); The Granger Collection,
New York: 25 (Francis Bicknell Carpenter), 4 bottom, 46 (Alonzo Chappel),
21 (Reynolds Jones), 4 top, 7, 8, 11, 12, 13 bottom, 18, 30 bottom, 31, 33, 34,
35, 36, 42, 49, 51, 53 left, 53 right, 58 bottom, 59 bottom.

# Did you know that studying history can be fun?

**BRING HISTORY TO LIFE** by becoming a history investigator. Examine the evidence (primary and secondary source materials); cross-examine the people and witnesses. Take a look at what was happening at the time—but be careful! What happened years ago might suddenly become incredibly interesting and change the way you think!

# Contents

4

# A House Divided

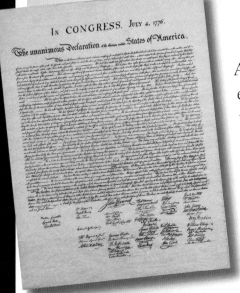

**The Declaration of Independence proclaims the idea that all men are created equal.**

America's **Founding Fathers** envisioned a united nation in which "all men are created equal" when they adopted the Declaration of Independence in 1776. The document put forth the idea that men were "endowed by their Creator" with "unalienable rights." But the United States was divided in the years leading up to the Civil War. The Northern and Southern states disagreed about politics, morals, and the economy.

The South's economy depended heavily on exporting cotton. But the economy of New England was based on industry, manufacturing, and railroads. Taxes placed on foreign imports made domestic manufacturing profitable. This helped the North's economy to prosper.

The South's economy was very strong just before war broke out. Planters were wealthy. Cotton still made up more than one-half of all U.S. exports. But the North's population growth soon surpassed the South's. Politicians from the Southern states feared losing control of Congress and a decisive voice in the Supreme Court. To lose control of government decisions threatened the existence of slavery. Slavery was very important to the South's way of life.

It would take a determined man to deal with the division within America. He would need vision, tireless energy, and great humanity. That man was Abraham Lincoln.

**Abraham Lincoln's work as a lawyer helped prepare him for the responsibilities of being president of the United States.**

**THE GREAT EMANCIPATOR.**

# CHAPTER 1

# HUMBLE BEGINNINGS

This tiny log cabin in Kentucky is a representation of the home Lincoln was born in.

ABRAHAM LINCOLN'S RISE TO political importance had modest beginnings. His grandfather was also named Abraham Lincoln. He journeyed from Virginia to Kentucky with his wife and their children. A Shawnee Indian shot him in May 1786 as he planted corn with his three sons. The eldest son was named Mordecai. Mordecai shot the attacker and saved the life of his six-year-old brother, Thomas. Young Thomas was soon sent to work on other farms in the area. Thomas's son Abraham would later describe him as a "wandering, laboring boy."

## Where It All Began

Thomas Lincoln was a farmer in Kentucky before moving his family to Indiana in 1817. He also bought and sold land. He sold his first farm in December 1808 and purchased a second one near Elizabethtown. He built a small log cabin with a stone fireplace and dirt floor. Thomas and his wife, Nancy, moved into the cabin with their baby daughter. Abraham was born on February 12, 1809. The Lincolns moved to Knob Creek Valley two years later. There, young Abraham saw peddlers, preachers, soldiers returning home from the War of 1812, and slaves. All of these must have made a deep impression on the little boy.

The Lincolns moved in December 1816 to an area in Indiana north of the Ohio River. Land there was plentiful. Thomas was troubled by Kentucky's support of slavery. But the Northwest Ordinance of 1787 had outlawed slavery north of the Ohio River.

**Thomas Lincoln, Abraham's father, was a Kentucky farmer.**

Abraham learned farming and how to use an axe. He helped his father chop trees and build the family's new house. He also had several months of schooling in a one-room frontier schoolhouse. Lincoln later said that his total school education was less than a year. Instead, he read and taught himself from the small collection of books available to him. Then tragedy touched Lincoln's life. On October 5, 1818, his mother died from drinking poisonous milk. The family's cows had eaten poisonous white snakeroot, a type of weed. Abraham was heartbroken.

# YESTERDAY'S HEADLINES

The Second Great Awakening was a Christian religious revival during the early 19th century. Preachers, especially Methodist and Baptist, traveled through the frontier. They held meetings that lasted for days. These meetings encouraged people to worship Christ. The preachers often helped establish frontier churches before moving on. The **evangelists** preached the equality of all races and genders. There were several well-known female evangelists and black preachers. Many preachers supported the antislavery movement.

Thomas Lincoln struggled for a year to hold his family together. He then married Sarah Bush Johnston. She was a widow he had known during his time in

**Young Lincoln grieved the death of his mother.**

Elizabethtown. She made a good home for Abraham and his sister. She also had her own children. She encouraged Abraham to learn. But his father would rather see him working more. Abraham found time to do both. He split rails and worked during the day. He spent his nights reading all the books he could borrow.

## The Making of the Man

Lincoln read a wide variety of books. Each one broadened the youngster's understanding of people and the world. He was entertained by *Aesop's Fables* and learned from the morals of the stories. He memorized Psalms from the King James Version of the Bible. He also came to

**Lincoln's stepmother loved him and encouraged him to read books on many subjects.**

SPOTLIGHT ON

*Sarah Bush Johnston Lincoln*

Sarah Bush was born in Elizabethtown, Kentucky, on December 13, 1788. She married Daniel Johnston in 1806. They had three children. Johnston died 10 years later. This left Sarah a widowed mother in difficult circumstances. Thomas visited Sarah after his first wife died in 1818. He brought her back to Indiana with him. They married on December 2, 1819. Sarah's love and encouragement of Abraham's curiosity had a lasting impact on the future president.

**When Lincoln wasn't working he enjoyed reading late into the night by firelight.**

understand good and evil through the morality tales of John Bunyan's *The Pilgrim's Progress.*

## A FIRSTHAND LOOK AT
## LESSONS IN ELOCUTION

Abraham Lincoln's command of voice, gesture, posture, and language all served to make him an extraordinary speaker. His speeches were intelligent, polished, and artful. His debates with Stephen Douglas and his historic speeches at Cooper Union, Gettysburg, and his second inauguration are considered masterpieces of American **oratory**. One of Lincoln's main sources of inspiration was William Scott's *Lessons in Elocution*, published in 1820. See page 60 for a link to view a copy of this book.

But it was William Grimshaw's 1820 *History of the United States* that may have affected Lincoln most deeply. Grimshaw was an Irish immigrant. He did nothing to hide his hatred of slavery. He declared that Americans "place the last rivet in the chain." Grimshaw concluded the book by writing, "Let us not only declare by words, but demonstrate by our actions, that 'all men are created equal.'" Lincoln made these words the foundation upon which he built his life and his political career.

Lincoln began to work for other farmers at age 14. He was tall for his age and unusually strong. He had developed real skill with the axe. Land boundaries between farms were often in dispute. Lincoln split

**Lincoln worked hard on his family's land as well as for neighboring farmers.**

15

rails from sunup to sundown. They were used to build the fences that farmers needed. He also built a simple flatboat and ferried passengers across the Ohio River. He was once arrested for operating the boat without a license. A local justice of the peace dismissed the charges against Lincoln.

Abraham was 17 when his sister, Sarah, married and moved away. She died in childbirth two years later. She was just 21 years old. A family death had once again struck Abraham and deeply saddened him.

Lincoln's maturity and wisdom were tested and expanded as his knowledge grew. A store owner asked him to help his son pilot a flatboat to New Orleans

**Abe transports passengers on a flatboat.**

**Slaves worked loading and unloading goods from ships stopping at New Orleans.**

and arrange trades of goods. New Orleans was a culturally varied city. Slave markets were common there. Witnessing slavery firsthand made the practice far more distasteful to Lincoln than simply reading a passage from Grimshaw's book. Lincoln's experiences during his few days in New Orleans may have set the course of his life. He was only 19 years old. But he was seasoned by the loss of loved ones and years of hard work. Lincoln set his sights on shaping his destiny.

# CHAPTER 2

# A MAN OF VISION

Lincoln was a volunteer in the Illinois Militia during the Black Hawk War in 1832.

THOMAS LINCOLN MOVED
once again in the winter of 1830. Abraham was
now 21. He was no longer required by custom
to provide financial support to his father. He
considered going out on his own. But he resisted
the idea. He accompanied the family to the town
of Decatur, Illinois. There, he helped his father
build a new homestead. His hard work won the
respect of his new neighbors.

In 1831, he went to work in New Salem,
Illinois, for businessman Denton Offutt. Lincoln
would spend the next six years in New Salem. He
was on his own at last.

**Working as a general store clerk was one of the many jobs Lincoln held in New Salem, Illinois.**

## A Date with Destiny

Lincoln's first years of independence were a time of wandering. He worked as a store clerk, a mill hand, a partner in a failed general store, a surveyor, and a postmaster of New Salem. He was also a **militia** captain during the Black Hawk War in 1832. The war was fought between Native Americans and the U.S. government over disputed lands given to the United States by the Indians decades earlier.

Lincoln had become interested in politics. He campaigned for a seat in the Illinois General Assembly in 1832. Lincoln promised improvements in roads, rivers, and canals. He was not elected. But he received more than 90 percent of the vote in New Salem. He was known and respected there. He campaigned again in 1834 and won easily.

Lincoln fell in love with Ann Rutledge. Ann was the daughter of New Salem's cofounder. She intended to marry Lincoln by 1835. But she died from **typhoid** fever. Combined with the early and unexpected deaths of his mother and sister, the tragedy sent Lincoln into a lengthy depression.

Lincoln had begun studying law. He started with William Blackstone's *Commentaries on the Laws of England*. Lincoln became a lawyer in 1837 after passing the Illinois bar exam. He would also be reelected to the Illinois legislature in 1836, 1838, and 1840. He

**Lincoln was elected to the Illinois General Assembly four times.**

**The Lincoln-Herndon Law Offices building still stands in Springfield, Illinois.**

campaigned each time as Sangamon County's Whig party candidate. He began to form his ideas and speak about his stance on the issue of slavery. That stance put him at odds with both Northern and Southern Democrats and Northern **abolitionists**. Lincoln was morally opposed to slavery. But he did not think that abolition was a workable alternative.

Lincoln moved to Springfield, Illinois, in 1837. He began a law practice there. He became partners with other lawyers and developed a successful business.

Lincoln met Mary Todd in summer 1839. She was the daughter of a prominent banker from Lexington, Kentucky. She was in some ways Lincoln's exact opposite. She was a privileged, well-educated child of a wealthy, slaveholding family. But she was also a Whig and keenly interested in education. Marriage seemed certain by January 1, 1841. But they suddenly broke up. Lincoln was plunged into despair. He missed days in the legislature. Mary was also upset. They eventually reunited and were married on November 4, 1842.

## Family and Career

In 1844, Lincoln partnered with Kentucky-born William Herndon in a Springfield law practice. The Lincolns purchased a house near the law office. Mary quickly adapted to her role as wife and soon as a mother. Lincoln threw himself into his work. He had partnered with Stephen T. Logan in 1841. Logan was respected for his thorough research and preparation. Lincoln was a self-taught lawyer. He learned much about law from Logan. Lincoln became more aware of researching legal cases and expressing his position clearly and concisely. His intelligence, honesty, and sense of fairness won him respect from other lawyers.

Lincoln's duties as a **circuit lawyer** expanded when he began his partnership with Herndon. As a circuit lawyer, he traveled extensively throughout central Illinois and represented a variety of clients. Lincoln formed political friendships with circuit judges. Many of them shared his views on slavery. Much of his work came from transportation lawsuits. These grew in number and complexity as the railroads expanded and the frontier moved westward. Lincoln sometimes represented people accused of murder. His practice and knowledge grew. His reputation thrust him into national attention. Lincoln was elected to a single term in the U.S. House of Representatives in 1846.

**Lincoln's partner, William Herndon, was a lawyer from Kentucky.**

Lincoln worked hard to provide for Mary and their sons. Robert was born in 1843. Edward was born in 1846 but died a month before his fourth birthday. Mary and Abraham looked to each other for support in their time of loss. Some of the pain of Edward's untimely passing was eased by the birth of Willie less than 11 months later. A fourth son, named Tad was born in 1853. Lincoln's time working away from home kept him from developing a close relationship with Robert. But he was deeply devoted to his two younger sons.

# TODAY'S PERSPECTIVE

Medical historians have speculated in recent years about the early deaths of Lincoln's sons. Only Robert, his firstborn, lived past the age of 18. Their deaths have traditionally been attributed to infectious diseases. Eddie was believed to have died from tuberculosis, Willie from typhoid fever, and Tad from "compression of the heart" due to infection. Infectious diseases and high childhood death rates in 19th-century America were common. But today's doctors have examined the family's medical records. They now see evidence of a rare genetic cancer called MEN2b. They believe Lincoln also suffered from the disorder.

# CHAPTER 3

# THE MAKING OF A PRESIDENT

Abraham Lincoln poses for a portrait. He earned a name for himself as a lawyer, a legislator, and an orator.

LINCOLN WAS NOW OUT OF politics and practicing law full-time. He thirsted for something that would make men "remember that he had lived." The opportunity presented itself in the hotly debated Kansas-Nebraska Act of 1854. Democratic senator Stephen A. Douglas of Illinois designed the pro-slavery act. It gave voters in the new territories of Kansas and Nebraska the right to decide whether they would have slavery. The act became law in May 1854. It threatened to extend the reach of slavery and the power of the slave states. Lincoln once again entered the political arena.

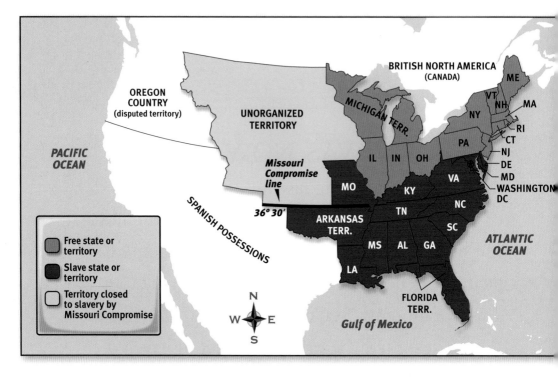

**As a result of the Missouri Compromise, slavery was not allowed in territories north of the 36°30' latitude.**

# Facing the Scourge of Slavery

On October 16, 1854, in Peoria, Illinois, Lincoln delivered a three-hour speech detailing his legal, economic, and moral objections to slavery and the Kansas-Nebraska Act. He began by expressing his concerns about the legality of the act. Giving voters absolute power in determining the issue of slavery in the new territories would raise the possibility of legalizing slavery north of the 36°30' latitude established by the 1820 Missouri Compromise. The Kansas-Nebraska Act was a **repeal** of this existing law. Lincoln pointed out slavery's inconsistency with the

# A FIRSTHAND LOOK AT
## THOMAS JEFFERSON'S LETTER

The 1820 Missouri Compromise was an agreement between congressional pro-slavery and antislavery groups to regulate the spread of slavery in frontier territories. It outlawed slavery north of the 36°30' latitude. But drawing this geographical line between slave and non-slave states was not favored by several influential congressmen. On April 22, 1820, Thomas Jefferson wrote to politician John Holmes. He expressed his concerns that extending slavery was "like a fire bell in the night." See page 60 for a link to view Jefferson's original letter.

Declaration of Independence and its assertion that "all men are created equal."

Lincoln's speech-making skills and righteous beliefs captured the imagination of those in attendance in Peoria. But he failed several months later in his attempt for a U.S. Senate seat in the 1854 election. The Whig party had been weakened by internal differences and could not get the needed votes. Lincoln responded by helping to establish the Republican Party.

The sharp division between Lincoln's moderate Republican beliefs and those of Southern Democrats grew deeper after the U.S. Supreme Court's 1857 ruling in *Dred Scott v. Sanford*. The decision upheld the legality of slavery. It also went further in denying slaves constitutional rights and U.S. citizenship. The court's ruling also questioned Congress's right to prohibit slavery in federal territories.

# YESTERDAY'S HEADLINES

The 1857 *Dred Scott* decision satisfied slaveholders because it removed all blocks to the expansion of slavery into federal territories while claiming that slaves could never be U.S. citizens. The Republicans in the North were outraged. An editorial in the Republican *Albany Evening Journal* on March 9, 1857, characterized the decision as an "issue forced upon us."

The ruling shocked Lincoln.

Lincoln was nominated by his party for a U.S. Senate seat in the 1858 election. But he failed to defeat Stephen Douglas. Lincoln's speeches and debates with Douglas clearly set forth his position on slavery. Lincoln delivered his famous "House Divided" speech in

**The *Dred Scott* case was argued before the Supreme Court in 1857.**

**During Lincoln's seven debates with Stephen Douglas he made his position on slavery clear to voters.**

Springfield, Illinois, on June 16, 1858. Lincoln echoed the New Testament when he said, "A house divided against itself cannot stand." Douglas had sought compromise between slave and free states. But Lincoln felt that compromise was not possible. The Union could not be preserved if it was divided over such a fundamental issue. It would eventually become all slave or all free states.

**The Lincoln-Douglas debates were held between August and October 1858.**

## A Voice in the Wilderness

The seven debates between Lincoln and Douglas from August 21 to October 15, 1858, took place only in Illinois. But they sent shock waves across the country. Douglas asserted the right of voters in frontier territories to decide whether they wanted those territories to be slave or free. Lincoln spoke against the *Dred Scott* decision. He carefully expressed his concern that accepting Douglas's ideas meant nationalizing slavery.

The newspaper coverage was extraordinary. People traveled from neighboring states just to hear the two candidates speak. Lincoln lost the race for the Senate seat. But he became so widely known that he immediately became a front-runner for the 1860 presidential race.

A group of prominent Republicans invited Lincoln to speak at Cooper Union in New York City on February

**This political cartoon illustrates Lincoln and Douglas battling for the presidency in 1860.**

**Slaves cut and gather sugarcane on a plantation. The Southern states argued that slavery was a necessary part of the farming industry.**

27, 1860. Lincoln began by establishing a historical perspective for the institution of slavery. He reached back to the intentions of the nation's Founding Fathers. Then he pointed out the differences between the Republican Party and the uprising led by abolitionist John Brown at Harpers Ferry, Virginia, the previous

October. Lincoln reminded his audience that he wished only to halt the spread of slavery into new territories. He did not want to abolish it. He also said that the Southern states' threat to leave the Union was a tactic meant to weaken support for the Republican Party.

Lincoln's Cooper Union speech was a huge success. But the raid at Harpers Ferry had stirred up sentiment among the **secessionists**. It also made the Union

**SPOTLIGHT ON**

### John Brown

Abolitionist John Brown briefly captured a federal arsenal at Harpers Ferry, Virginia, in October 1859 with the help of about two dozen followers. He planned to arm slaves throughout the South and free them. The uprising failed. His group was captured by the U.S. Army under Robert E. Lee. Lee later became a leading general in the **Confederate States of America**. Brown was put on trial. He was found guilty of **treason** and hanged.

more fragile. Lincoln was viewed in the South as an abolitionist rather than as a moderate Republican. He struck fear into the hearts of slaveholders. He won the 1860 presidential election. But he was not on the ballot in 10 Southern states. They claimed he did not represent them. The foundation of the Founding Fathers' vision of America was about to unravel as Lincoln took office in March 1861.

# CHAPTER 4

# TRIAL BY FIRE

Abraham Lincoln
was inaugurated as
president of the United
States on March 4, 1861.

SOUTH CAROLINA SECEDED, or withdrew, from the Union on December 20, 1860. Lincoln had not yet assumed office. Mississippi, Florida, Alabama, Georgia, Louisiana, and Texas followed in the next six weeks. The seven states formed the Confederate States of America on February 4, 1861. They flew their own flag and printed their own money. They also created their own constitution and had their own legislature. Jefferson Davis was named president of the Confederacy. The United States was moving ever closer to a civil war.

**Before Lincoln took office, Jefferson Davis became president of the Confederate States of America, a group of Southern states that had withdrawn from the Union.**

## War

Lincoln's diplomacy was tested almost immediately. Fort Sumter was located near Charleston, South Carolina. It was still under the command of U.S. major Robert Anderson. But the rest of Charleston had been claimed by the Confederacy. Anderson requested that Lincoln resupply the fort. The president notified South Carolina's governor of his peaceful intentions. The governor demanded that the federal troops leave the fort at once.

Anderson refused to leave. The Confederates opened fire on the fort on April 12, 1861. Anderson was outgunned. He quickly surrendered. There was now considerable support for war in both the North and the South. Lincoln called on Northern states to supply militias to defend Washington and end the uprising.

The Battle of Fort Sumter begins, marking the start of the Civil War.

**President Lincoln met with General George McClellan during the Civil War.**

Virginia, Arkansas, Tennessee, and North Carolina seceded and joined the Confederacy in response.

Lincoln took an active role in command of the Union war effort. He started by establishing a blockade of Southern ports. The blockade ruined the Confederacy's ability to support the war. It also discouraged the British from becoming involved. Lincoln made it clear that support or recognition of the Confederacy was a declaration of war against the United States.

Lincoln spent 42 days at the battlefront during the war. He replaced ineffective military commanders with those who had proved themselves worthy in combat. Generals who failed to fight aggressively were replaced with those who would. Lincoln studied war tactics and battle strategy from books at the Library of Congress. He communicated often with commanders at the battlefront.

General Ulysses S. Grant's siege of Vicksburg, Mississippi, in the summer of 1863 was a major strategic victory for the Union forces. It also convinced Lincoln of Grant's leadership abilities. Lincoln made him the commanding officer of all Union forces. This would be a major reason for the Union's victory. Confederate forces surrendered to Grant at Appomattox Court House, Virginia, on April 9, 1865.

**Union leaders (from left to right) William Tecumseh Sherman, Ulysses S. Grant, Lincoln, and David Dixon Porter review military strategy.**

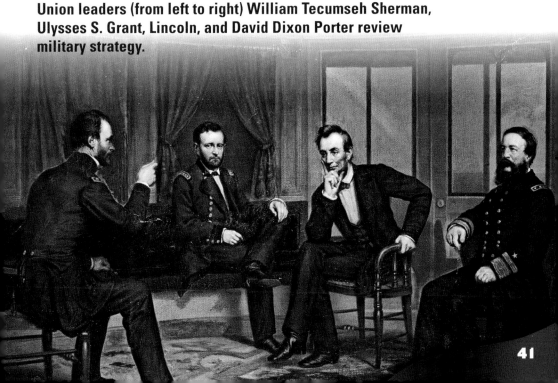

President Lincoln delivered his now-famous Gettysburg Address on November 19, 1863.

## A Man of Sorrows

Lincoln's presence at the front and frequent communication with the troops made the horrors of war a living reality for the president. He spoke with the men and saw the wounded in army hospitals. He experienced loss the same way thousands of his soldiers did. He gave a speech in Gettysburg, Pennsylvania, on November 19, 1863, to dedicate the new National Cemetery. The cemetery was the final resting ground for the soldiers who fought and died at the historic battle that had taken place there in July of that year. An audience of about 15,000 heard the president speak. His words were few but eloquent. They served as a reminder of what the soldiers had fought so bravely to preserve.

Lincoln also experienced personal losses during the war years. He was informed in October 1861 that his longtime friend Edward Baker had died in an attack against the Confederates at Ball's Bluff, Virginia. Baker had been a fellow legislator in Illinois years before. Lincoln was so fond of his friend that he had named his son Eddie after him. Baker had visited Lincoln at the White House the day before he died. Willie Lincoln died of typhoid fever exactly four months later.

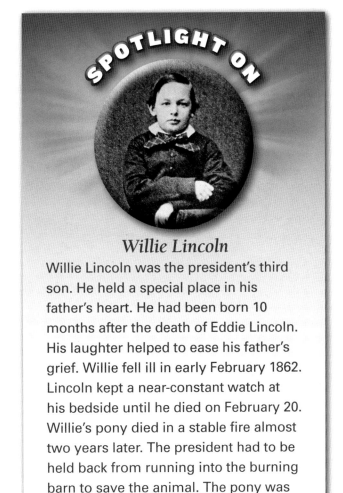

### SPOTLIGHT ON

**Willie Lincoln**

Willie Lincoln was the president's third son. He held a special place in his father's heart. He had been born 10 months after the death of Eddie Lincoln. His laughter helped to ease his father's grief. Willie fell ill in early February 1862. Lincoln kept a near-constant watch at his bedside until he died on February 20. Willie's pony died in a stable fire almost two years later. The president had to be held back from running into the burning barn to save the animal. The pony was all Lincoln had to remind him of his boy.

# CHAPTER 5

# THE MAKING OF A LEGEND

Lincoln takes a quiet moment to think.

LINCOLN WAGED POLITICAL
battles with both his foes and his supporters
during the war. Radical Republicans wanted to see
him push to abolish slavery at once. But Lincoln
knew that abruptly doing so would drive the
border states of Delaware, Kentucky, Maryland,
and Missouri into the Confederacy. These four
states were slave states. But they had not seceded
from the Union. Northern Democrats pushed
him to compromise with the Confederates. The
Confederates hated Lincoln and wished him dead.
Lincoln knew compromise had failed in the past.

**President Lincoln conferred with his top advisers before delivering the Emancipation Proclamation.**

Lincoln waited for an opportunity to address the issue of slavery head-on. Lincoln saw his opportunity when the Union turned back a Confederate advance at the Battle of Antietam in September 1862. He issued the Emancipation Proclamation on January 1, 1863. It announced the freedom of most of the nation's slaves.

# A FIRSTHAND LOOK AT

## THE EMANCIPATION PROCLAMATION

The Emancipation Proclamation is one of the United States' most important documents. It is now preserved in the National Archives in Washington, D.C. The proclamation linked the Union war effort to a strong moral cause. It transformed a war to save the Union into a war of liberation and freedom. See page 60 for a link to view the original handwritten document.

## The Last Casualty of the War

The evening of April 14, 1865, was to have been one of quiet celebration for Lincoln. The Confederates had surrendered to General Grant five days earlier. This all but brought the Civil War to a close. Lincoln and his wife planned a relaxing evening at Ford's Theatre

**Ford's Theatre was rebuilt in 1863 after a fire destroyed the original building.**

# YESTERDAY'S HEADLINES

The Confederate capital, Richmond, Virginia, was evacuated with the advance of the Union army in the final days of the war. Warehouses and supplies were burned. The fire raged out of control. It turned the factories and houses along the James River to ash. Richmond resident Sally Putnam described the "roaring, crackling and hissing of the flames, the bursting of shells at the Confederate Arsenal, the sounds of the Instruments of martial music, the neighing of the horses, the shoutings of the multitudes."

in Washington, D.C. They planned to see a comedy called *Our American Cousin.*

John Wilkes Booth planned a different end to Lincoln's evening. Booth was an actor and a Confederate supporter. Booth and several accomplices had planned for months to kidnap Lincoln. But those plans fell through. Booth had now become **obsessed** with killing Lincoln. Lincoln had just been elected to a second term as president. He had delivered his second inaugural speech about six weeks earlier. Booth was in the crowd listening to Lincoln's words about healing the divided nation.

**John Wilkes Booth jumped from the theater balcony and onto the stage after shooting President Lincoln.**

Booth's opportunity had finally arrived. He slid into the president's box during a break in the play and shot Lincoln in the back of the head. Lincoln was carried to the bedroom of William Petersen's boardinghouse across

# YESTERDAY'S HEADLINES

Lincoln delivered his second inaugural address on March 4, 1865. An editorial in the *New York Times* on April 17 reflected back on the speech. It noted how Lincoln's words were about justice, forgiveness, and humanity. It was not the speech of a conquering hero. It was the speech of a religious prophet. English and French critics disliked its religious tone. But it seemed true to Lincoln's character that his words swelled with compassion for "all of the wrongs done to the helpless race.

the street. Several doctors attended him. But the president's condition was hopeless. Abraham Lincoln lost his final battle at 7:22 a.m. on April 15, 1865. He was the last casualty of the war.

## Long Journey Home

A memorial service was held four days after Lincoln's death in Washington, D.C. Some 25,000 people attended. On April 21, a train carrying Lincoln's body began the long journey to Springfield, Illinois. Lincoln was to be buried there. The journey took nearly two weeks and covered almost 1,700 miles (2,700 km). The train stopped in 180 cities and towns along the way to give residents a chance to pay their respects to the president. The train arrived in Springfield on May 3. Lincoln's body was placed in its tomb on May 4. It remains there today.

**After a two-week journey from Washington, D.C., Abraham Lincoln was buried in Springfield, Illinois.**

# What Happened Where?

**Decatur, Illinois** In 1830, the family moved to Decatur, Illinois.

Chicago

IL

IN

**New Salem, Illinois** In July 1831, Abraham struck out on his own and moved to New Salem. There, he worked as a clerk, store owner, and postmaster, and began his study of law.

New Salem

Decatur

Springfield

Indianapolis

**Springfield, Illinois** Lincoln arrived in Springfield on April 15, 1837, to begin his law practice. On February 11, 1861, he left Springfield on a train headed east to Washington, D.C., where he was sworn in as the 16th president of the United States on March 4.

Gentryville   KY

Hodgenville

**Gentryville, in Spencer County, Indiana** The Lincolns moved to Indiana in December 1816, settling near present-day Gentryville.

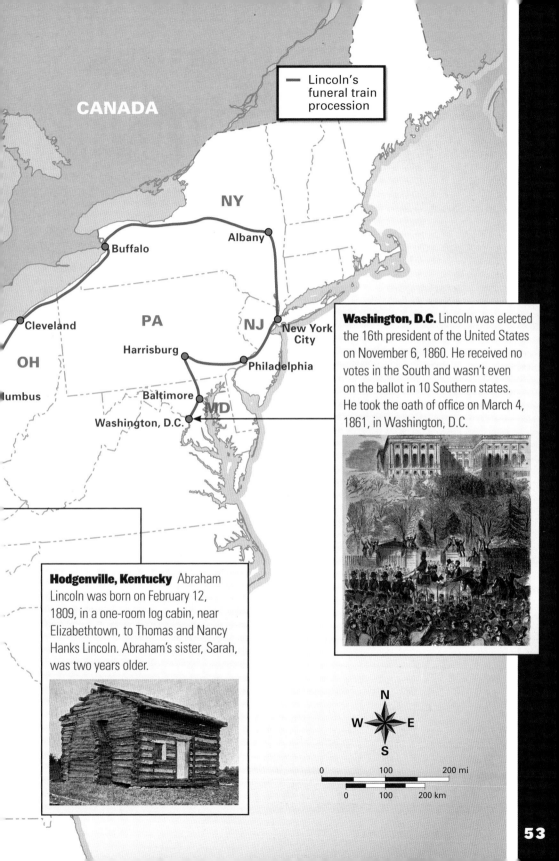

CANADA

NY

— Lincoln's funeral train procession

Buffalo

Albany

Cleveland

PA

NJ

OH

Harrisburg

New York City

Columbus

Baltimore

Philadelphia

MD

Washington, D.C.

**Washington, D.C.** Lincoln was elected the 16th president of the United States on November 6, 1860. He received no votes in the South and wasn't even on the ballot in 10 Southern states. He took the oath of office on March 4, 1861, in Washington, D.C.

**Hodgenville, Kentucky** Abraham Lincoln was born on February 12, 1809, in a one-room log cabin, near Elizabethtown, to Thomas and Nancy Hanks Lincoln. Abraham's sister, Sarah, was two years older.

N
W E
S

0    100    200 mi

0    100    200 km

# A New Birth of Freedom

**Today, people from around the world remember Abraham Lincoln by visiting the Lincoln Memorial in Washington, D.C.**

Abraham Lincoln's message to us lives in his words and in the courage and wisdom that guided him throughout his life. But his legacy is not limited to the geographical

**AROUND 3.5 MILLION PEOPLE VISIT**

boundaries of the United States. His Gettysburg Address borrowed from the Declaration of Independence and proclaimed that "all men are created equal." Lincoln did not intend his words to be true only for Americans. He intended them to be true for all people.

Countless people around the world have fought for equal rights and freedom in the 150 years since Lincoln spoke those words. They struggle for the chance to experience their "unalienable rights" of "life, liberty and the pursuit of happiness" as the Founding Fathers envisioned almost 240 years ago.

Lincoln was a hero to many leaders of rights movements all over the world. Nelson Mandela of South Africa looked to him as a role model. Lincoln has been described by world leaders as "a humanitarian as broad as the world" and someone who "regarded the whole world as his native land." Several African nations put his image on their postage stamps when they won their freedom from colonial rulers.

In 2011, civil unrest in nations such as Libya, Egypt, Bahrain, Yemen, Iran, Algeria, and Saudi Arabia focused the world's attention on civil rights abuses, lack of political freedoms, and discrimination. It would not be surprising if Lincoln's idea of "government of the people, by the people, for the people" echoed in the cries of protesters in these many lands.

THE LINCOLN MEMORIAL EACH YEAR.

# INFLUENTIAL INDIVIDUALS

**Thomas Lincoln** (1778–1851) was a farmer, landowner, and the father of Abraham Lincoln.

**Nancy Hanks Lincoln** (1784–1818) was Abraham's mother who died from contaminated milk.

**Sarah Bush Johnston Lincoln** (1788–1869) was Thomas Lincoln's second wife and Abraham's stepmother.

**John Brown** (1800–1859) was a Northern abolitionist who led a raid on the federal arsenal at Harpers Ferry, Virginia, in October 1859. He was captured and hanged for treason.

**Stephen Logan** (1800–1880) was one of Lincoln's Springfield, Illinois, law partners.

**Robert E. Lee** (1807–1870) was the commander of the Army of North Virginia and commanding general of the Confederate armies in the last weeks of the war.

**Jefferson Davis** (1808–1889) was president of the Confederate States of America during the Civil War.

**Abraham Lincoln** (1809–1865) was the 16th president of the United States and Union leader during the American Civil War. He was assassinated less than one week after the war ended.

Jefferson Davis

**Edward Baker** (1811–1861) was a U.S. congressman from Illinois and a close friend of Lincoln's. He was killed at the Battle of Ball's Bluff in the first year of the war.

**Stephen Douglas** (1813–1861) was a Democratic senator from Illinois. He was the author of the Kansas-Nebraska Act of 1854 and Lincoln's opponent in many historic debates.

Stephen Douglas

**Mary Todd Lincoln** (1818–1882) was the daughter of a Lexington, Kentucky, slaveholder and wife of Abraham Lincoln.

**William Herndon** (1818–1891) was Lincoln's junior partner at the Springfield, Illinois, law office and his biographer.

**Ulysses S. Grant** (1822–1885) was a Union general who accepted General Robert E. Lee's surrender at Appomattox to end the Civil War. He was elected the 18th president of the United States in 1868.

**John Wilkes Booth** (1838–1865) was an American actor, a Confederate supporter, and the assassin of Abraham Lincoln.

John Wilkes Booth

**Robert, Edward, William, and Thomas Lincoln** were the sons of Abraham and Mary Todd Lincoln. Only Robert survived to adulthood.

# TIMELINE

| 1809 | 1816 | 1818 | 1819 | 1831 |
|------|------|------|------|------|
| **February 12** Abraham Lincoln born in Kentucky | Lincoln's family moves to Indiana | Lincoln's mother, Nancy Hanks Lincoln, dies | Lincoln's father marries Sarah Bush Johnston | Lincoln leaves for New Salem, Illinois |

| 1854 | 1857 | 1858 | 1860 | 1861–1865 |
|------|------|------|------|-----------|
| Kansas-Nebraska Act approved | *Dred Scott* decision made | Lincoln debates Stephen Douglas; loses his bid for the U.S. Senate | Lincoln speaks at Cooper Union; wins the presidential election | American Civil War fought |

**1832**

**1834–1842**

**1837**

**1842**

**1844**

Lincoln serves as a militia captain in the Black Hawk War

Lincoln serves in the Illinois General Assembly

Lincoln admitted to Illinois Bar Association

Lincoln weds Mary Todd

Lincoln partners with William Herndon

**1863**

**1865**

**January 1**
Emancipation Proclamation issued

**November 19**
Lincoln delivers the Gettysburg Address

**April 9**
Robert E. Lee surrenders at Appomattox Court House

**April 14**
Lincoln assassinated at Ford's Theatre

# LIVING HISTORY

Primary sources provide firsthand evidence about a topic. Witnesses to a historical event create primary sources. They include autobiographies, newspaper reports of the time, oral histories, photographs, and memoirs. A secondary source analyzes primary sources, and is one step or more removed from the event. Secondary sources include textbooks, encyclopedias, and commentaries.

**The Emancipation Proclamation** The Emancipation Proclamation was President Lincoln's courageous attempt to liberate slaves in the United States. To see a copy of one of history's most important documents, go to *www.archives.gov/exhibits/featured_ documents/emancipation_proclamation/*

**Fort Sumter Letters** To see the contents of the letters exchanged by Union major Robert Anderson and Confederate general Pierre Beauregard the day before the attack on Fort Sumter, go to *www. nytimes.com/1861/04/29/news/the-fort-sumter-correspondence.html*

**Lincoln's Law Office** The building where Lincoln and William Herndon practiced law in Springfield, Illinois, still stands as a preserved historic site. You can read about and see the building at *http://showcase.netins.net/web/creative/lincoln/sites/law.htm*

**Thomas Jefferson's Letter** You can view Jefferson's original handwritten letter at *www.loc.gov/exhibits/jefferson/images/vc159.jpg*

**William Scott's *Lessons in Elocution*** You can see a copy of the *Lessons in Elocution* at *http://books.google.com/ books?hl=en&id=L1gCAAAAYAAJ*

## Books

Colbert, David. *Abraham Lincoln*. New York: Aladdin Books, 2009.

Haugen, Brenda. *Abraham Lincoln: Great American President*. Minneapolis: Compass Point Books, 2006.

Stone, Tanya Lee. *Abraham Lincoln*. New York: DK Biography, 2005.

Swanson, James L. *Chasing Lincoln's Killer*. New York: Scholastic Press, 2009.

Venezia, Mike. *Abraham Lincoln: Sixteenth President*. New York: Children's Press, 2005.

## Web Sites

### Abraham Lincoln Online

*http://showcase.netins.net/web/creative/lincoln.html*

Check out this huge collection of speeches, writings, educational resources, interviews with historians, events, and books—all devoted to Abraham Lincoln.

### Abraham Lincoln Presidential Library and Museum

*www.alplm.org*

Here you'll find numerous exhibits and historical settings, including full-scale dioramas of key areas of the Lincoln White House, his box at Ford's Theatre, and his boyhood home. The original Gettysburg Address and a signed copy of the Emancipation Proclamation are also on display.

### Lincoln Home National Historic Site

*www.nps.gov/liho/index.htm*

Take virtual tours of the Lincoln home and neighborhood in Springfield, Illinois.

# GLOSSARY

**abolitionists** (ab-uh-LISH-uh-nists) people in favor of immediately ending slavery

**circuit lawyer** (SUR-kit LAW-yur) a lawyer who travels over a territory and argues cases in different locations

**Confederate States of America** (kuhn-FED-ur-uht STATES UV uh-MER-uh-kuh) a group of 11 Southern states that wanted to preserve slavery and seceded from the United States for the duration of the Civil War

**elocution** (eh-lo-KUE-shuhn) the art of speaking well in public

**evangelists** (ee-VAN-jel-ists) preachers of the Christian gospel

**Founding Fathers** (FOUND-ihng FAH-thurz) the leading figures in the creation of the United States

**militia** (muh-LISH-uh) a group of people who are trained to fight but who aren't professional soldiers

**obsessed** (uhb-SESSD) thinking about something all the time

**oratory** (OR-uh-tore-ee) the art of speaking in public

**repeal** (ri-PEEL) the act of officially doing away with something

**secessionists** (si-SEH-shuhn-ihsts) people wanting their state to withdraw from the United States

**treason** (TREE-zuhn) the crime of betraying one's own country

**typhoid** (TYE-foid) an infectious disease with symptoms of high fever that can lead to death

# INDEX

Page numbers in *italics* indicate illustrations.

# ABOUT THE AUTHOR

**Peter Benoit** is a graduate of Skidmore College in Saratoga Springs, New York. His degree is in mathematics. He has been a tutor and educator for many years. Peter has written more than two dozen books for Children's Press. He has written about ecosystems, disasters, and Native Americans, among other topics. He is also the author of more than 2,000 poems. His lifelong interest in Abraham Lincoln began at age six, when he memorized Lincoln's Gettysburg Address.